D1790875

PARAMAHANSA YOGANANDA
(1893–1952)

Remolding Your Life

by
Paramahansa Yogananda

"How-to-Live" Series

No. 1709

Self-Realization Fellowship
FOUNDED 1920
Paramahansa Yogananda

A publication of
SELF-REALIZATION FELLOWSHIP
Founded in 1920 by Paramahansa Yogananda

ABOUT THE "HOW-TO-LIVE" SERIES: These informal talks and essays were originally published by Self-Realization Fellowship in its quarterly magazine, *Self-Realization*. Some have also appeared in anthologies and on recordings produced by the society. The "How-to-Live" series was created in response to requests from readers for pocket-size booklets presenting Paramahansa Yogananda's teachings on various subjects. The series offers guidance by Sri Yogananda and some of his longtime disciples, members of the monastic Self-Realization Order, many of whom had the opportunity to receive the spiritual direction and training of this beloved world teacher over a period of many years. New titles are added to the series periodically.

Authorized by the International Publications Council of
SELF-REALIZATION FELLOWSHIP
3880 San Rafael Avenue • Los Angeles, CA 90065-3219

Self-Realization Fellowship was founded by Paramahansa Yogananda as the instrument for the worldwide dissemination of his teachings. The Self-Realization Fellowship name and emblem (shown above) appear on all SRF books, recordings, and other publications, assuring the reader that a work originates with the society established by Paramahansa Yogananda and faithfully conveys his teachings.

ISBN-13: 978-0-87612-399-7
ISBN-10: 0-87612-399-X
Printed in the United States of America on recycled paper ♻
1709-J4043

— ✧ —

*There is a Power that will light
your way to health, happiness,
peace, and success, if you will but
turn toward that Light.*

— PARAMAHANSA YOGANANDA

— ✧ —

Remolding Your Life

By Paramahansa Yogananda

*A talk given at the
Self-Realization Fellowship Temple,
Hollywood, California, January 3, 1943*

Today's subject is a very important one. Everything you hear this morning you should strive to remember and put into practice. It is so easy to be inspired momentarily, and then forget much of what you heard. That is why I often employ repetition; for to penetrate the hard core of human consciousness, a truth must be repeated again and again. By such review, it gradually becomes a habitual part of one's thoughts.

There is a vast difference between just listening to a lecture and applying the truths it contains. Everything my Guru* [Swami Sri Yukteswar] told me I put into practice. As a result of his training I have always kept

* See glossary.

my spiritual priorities straight. I never miss
three things: my meditations, morning and
night; my exercises;* and service to others.
These I religiously perform; all else of less
importance I somehow manage.

Living in the consciousness of God, I find
many things that once seemed necessary
have become unnecessary. Last night I felt
no need for sleep because my awareness of
God was so strong. Once in a while I would
see my body asleep, but that subconscious
sleep-*samadhi* (*nidra samadhi sthiti*) soon
slipped away and my mind and body were
filled solely with the consciousness of God.

These things that I tell you come from
my own direct experience; and one day they
will be a part of your realization. Through
Him whom I perceive within, it is possible
to transmit to those who are in tune the
light of God that is in me. It is not I, but

* The Energization Exercises, formulated by Paramahansa Yogananda and taught in the *Self-Realization
Fellowship Lessons.*

He who is in me whom I extol. Just as the wealthy man can bestow his fortune on his worthy children, so it is possible for the man of spiritual wealth to bequeath his divine riches to those disciples who follow his example. This is true of all great masters. There are many instances of this transmission of spiritual consciousness, such as the "mantle" of Elijah that fell on Elisha, and the Holy Ghost imparted by Christ to the faithful eleven of his twelve close disciples.

Many come to the spiritual path; but it is those who remain steadfast to the end who will enter the Kingdom of Heaven. True devotees—those who see that the murky paths of this world all lead to disillusionment—steadily pursue God, never doubting Him. It doesn't matter whether He answers or not. The devotee inwardly prays: "Lord, Thou knowest I am coming, so I care not when Thou wilt reply to me. Though I am undeserving of Thy response, yet Thou canst not refuse me when the time is right."

As soon as God is convinced that you are in earnest and nothing can turn you away from Him, then through the guru He gives you the final realization—the guru transmits to you the light of God that flows through him. Perhaps you thought you would never know such a blessing. That supreme experience I received from my Guru. He gave me by his touch what I could not attain by the power and effort of my meditations alone.

Beginning with this new year, make firm spiritual resolutions. I have made a few myself, and pray with all my heart that with the blessing of the Father and Gurudeva I will carry these through.

Life Is a Matrix of Consciousness

We are made of the matrix of consciousness. All life was spumed out of the one Source of the river of consciousness. Your individualized consciousness is thus the very foundation of your existence. All of your thoughts and actions are bubbles and droplets of the river of consciousness.

The seemingly solid body is actually a mass of electromagnetic currents. Its electrons and protons are condensations of the relative positive and negative creative thoughts projected by God, which I call thoughtrons. All creation derives from these thoughtrons, the consciousness of God.

What is the difference between black and white? They are two contrasting thoughts, each frozen into its particular concept, that is all. For example, black horses and white horses in a dream are nothing but different crystallizations, relativities of the dreamer's one stream of thought.

In the ultimate sense, then, all things are made of pure consciousness; their finite appearance is the result of the relativity of consciousness. Therefore, if you want to change anything in yourself, you must change the process of thought that occasions the materialization of consciousness into different forms of matter and action. That is the way, the only way, to remold your life.

The Tenacity of Habits

I can give a directive to my mind and it will at once react or behave accordingly. Most people who make up their minds to stop smoking or to stop eating so many sweets will continue with those actions in spite of themselves. They do not change because their minds, like blotting paper, have soaked up habits of thought. Habit means that the mind believes it cannot get rid of a particular thought.

Habit, indeed, is tenacious. Once you perform an action, it leaves an effect or impression on the consciousness. As a result of this influence, you are likely to repeat that action. After several repetitions, that inclination is so strengthened that the action becomes a habit. In some people, just one act is enough to form a habit, because of a latent predisposition from past lives.* The mind may tell you that you cannot free yourself from a particular habit; but habits are nothing but

* See *reincarnation* in glossary.

repetitions of your own thoughts, and these you have the capacity to change.

The nature of habit can be understood by this analogy: Clay can be molded into a vase; and while the clay is still soft it is easy to change the form of that vase again and again. But once it is fired in an oven, its shape becomes firmly set. So it is with your consciousness. Your thoughts are molding your actions, and your mental convictions from the repetition of those actions is the fire that hardens the thoughts into unyielding habit patterns.

Why are the faces of all of you different? Because your minds are different. Your habit patterns of thoughts have molded not only your mind but also your body. You have probably noticed that some thin people might eat five meals a day and yet never gain weight. And some heavy people may eat very little and yet become heavier. Why? The former, sometime in a past life, established the thought in their consciousness that they were thin, and in this life they brought that

thought and tendency with them. No matter
what they do, they never grow fat. It is the
same with obese persons. In past lives, they
left this world with the consciousness of being fat, and they brought the seed of that
thought into their present existence. The
whole physiology of the body responds to
these karmic seed tendencies.* If you want
to change your constitution, then you have
to say, "It is I who thought myself into being
thin (or heavy or sickly). Now I will myself
to be robust (or whatever you so desire)." If
you get rid of the thought that has made
you other than you want to be, you will see
the body change. I can maintain my weight,
or as easily be thin at will. My trouble as a
youth was that I was too thin. Master cured
me of that consciousness, so ever since I
have preferred to be heavier.

"Old Age" Is a State of Mind

Most people are psychological antiques;
they never change, year after year always

* See *karma* in glossary.

the same. Everyone has self-limiting idio-
syncrasies. These were not put into your nature by God, but were created by you. These
are what you must change—by remember-
ing that these habits, peculiar to your nature, are nothing but manifestations of your
own thoughts.

If you feel that your character is not
what you think it should be, remember that
it was molded by none other than yourself.
Certainly there are outside influences, but
inner acceptance is the determining factor. If
everyone says that Johnny is a bad boy, and
Johnny accepts that condemnation, he may
not make the effort to be good; he adopts
that negative thought. But if he had refused
to accept it, he could have been different.

One must never give up hope of becom-
ing better. A person is old only when he
refuses to make the effort to change. That
stagnant state is the only "old age" I recog-
nize. When a person says again and again,
"I can't change; this is the way I am," then

I have to say, "All right, stay that way, since you have made up your mind to be like that."

Try to be more pliable, like children. However, even some children are old before their time because they have lacked the training and have not been given the incentive to change past-life tendencies; their mental clay is already fired in the oven and they grow up with the same inclinations they had in childhood. On the other hand, there are aged people with whom I have talked, just once, and they have changed for the better. God is not a respecter of age, for the soul is ageless. Those who are always ready to improve and expand themselves are like receptive children. Those who grow in understanding become more childlike. The great masters are like that.

To be childlike doesn't mean one is wishy-washy. I am not afraid of anything in the world; no one can intimidate me. I live for God and truth, and I love everyone. If someone misunderstands me, I try to establish understanding. But if I cannot change that person, neither can I be moved by his bad behavior. If a nonunderstanding person has made up his mind against you, why should you change in order to please or placate him? Stand by your principles when you are right, and be willing instantly to change yourself when you are wrong.

Will Power Is the Instrument of Change

If you have molded clay into a vase and fired it, and now you want to make that object into a tray, you cannot do so. But you can pulverize the vase and add that powder to fresh clay, and then form it into a tray. Likewise, when a bad habit is fixed in your mind and you want to change it, you will have to use your strong will to pulverize that habit and absorb it into fresh, pliable good actions that can be remolded to the desired image. Strong will means strong conviction. The minute you say to yourself, "I am not bound by this habit," and mean it, the habit will be gone.

Look within and determine your main characteristics. Some love to write, or compose music, or dance; others enjoy finance and economics, and so on. Unfortunately, some love to gossip, and others to fight. Don't try to change in yourself what is good. But those things you do against your will, and that make you unhappy after you have done them, are what you want to get rid of. How? Affirm with conviction, before going to bed and on arising in the morning, "I can change. I have the will to change. I *will* change!" Hold to that thought throughout the day, and carry it with you into the subconscious land of sleep and the superconscious realm of meditation.

Suppose your problem is that you frequently get angry, and afterwards feel very sorry for having lost your temper. Every night and morning make up your mind to avoid anger, and then watch yourself carefully. The first day may be difficult, but the second may be a little easier. The third will be easier still. After a few days you will see that victory is possible. In a year, if you keep up your effort, you will be another person. In my childhood, I used to get angry at injustices. One day I saw how foolish it was: I could not change the world in a minute by a display of wrath. I raised my hands and vowed: "I will never be angry again." Since then, I have never been angry within, though I can be outwardly fiery when necessary.

When I came to America, twenty-some years ago, I saw everyone was drinking coffee; so I tasted it for the first time, and gradually came to like it. Lest it become a habit, I made a rule never to drink coffee by myself. Still, there were so many invitations that I found I was drinking coffee all the time. One day, as I ate alone in a restaurant, I realized I missed the coffee. I thought, "So! You got me! All right: good-bye, coffee habit!" That was the end of it; in the past twenty years I have never touched it. Just last night, some friends served coffee to me.

It tasted all right, but it will never again be tempting to me.

Freedom Is to Act for Your Highest Welfare

You must be free—unenslaved by habits, or the wish to please society, or anything else. To be able to do, not what you want to do but what you should do for your own highest welfare, that is freedom.

For example, temperamental people, addicted to their emotions, love to intimidate and "scare the daylights" out of others. I say, "Go ahead, if you must, but remember that *you* will have to pay for that bad behavior—no one else." Every wrong action goes against one's own well-being. It fails to give the peace and happiness expected. Sometimes it seems difficult to be good, while it is easy to be bad; and that to give up the bad things is to miss something. But I say you will not miss anything but sorrow.

Do not be like the naughty child who wants to do the very thing he is told not to do. Everything that the great ones have warned against is like poisoned honey. I say don't taste it. You may argue, "But it is sweet." Well, my reasoning is that after you have tasted the sweetness it will destroy you. Evil was made sweet to delude you. You have to use your discrimination to distinguish between poisoned honey and that which is in your best interest. Avoid those things that will ultimately hurt you, and choose those that will give you freedom and happiness.

In this new year, change your consciousness. Cultivate the right conduct and good habits that lead to freedom. When you can say, "I don't indulge in bad habits because they are against my interest; I choose goodness of my own free will," that is freedom; and that is what I want for you.

Both Discrimination and Will Power Are Necessary

Remolding your consciousness means exercising free will guided by discrimination and energized by will power. Discrimination is your keen eyesight and will is your power of locomotion. Without will, you may know what is right through discrimination and yet not act on it. It is acting on knowledge that gets you to your goal. So both discrimination and will are necessary.

Will power is easy to develop. Try first for small accomplishments. Gradually you will get rid of tendencies you thought you could not overcome. Watch your consciousness. Develop the habit of self-examination, of watching and analyzing your thoughts and behavior. When there are telltale signs of bad habits or inclinations, that is the time to discriminate and resist with will power.

The first time you succumbed to a temptation, you didn't expect that you would be compelled to repeat it. But after giving in a few times, habit took over. Eventually you felt you could not get rid of that habit. But you can, if you use your God-given discrimination and will power. Habits are simply thoughts grooved deeply into the brain. The needle of the mind plays those records of habits again and again. Even the chemistry of the body responds, as with addiction. Applying mind and will can change those patterns. Don't immediately attempt dramatic changes. Experiment in little things first, to train your inherent power of command. I see that a great many of you here today will be rid of your bad habits as a result of following these suggestions.

Think Away Undesirable Thoughts

Start the new year with the resolve to face your bad habits and conquer them. Take the bull by the horns, so to speak, and tame it. Your bad habits are the satanic influence that has kept God out of your life.

Good habits can be compared to good people. When they look through the window of your mind, they see they cannot get into your life because the chairs of your consciousness are occupied by bad habits. Evict the undesirable occupants and let the noble ones in. You don't need the help of

anything or anyone else to change yourself;
just change your consciousness. Very simply, all you have to do is to think away the
thoughts you want to destroy, by replacing
them with constructive thoughts. This is the
key to heaven; it is in your hands.

Those people who behave in the same
way day in and day out are the ones who
refuse to change their thoughts. That is
all. There is a saying: "A woman convinced
against her will is of the same opinion
still." Why say this of woman? Man is the
same. Everyone must learn to cut out wrong
thoughts with the incisive scalpel of wisdom. Thought is a projection of God's om-
nipotent light and will. If you make up your
mind to change, you can use its power to
transform yourself.

We Are What We Think We Are

We are what we *think* we are. The habitual inclination of our thoughts deter-
mines our talents and abilities, and our
personality. Thus, some *think* they are

writers or artists, industrious or lazy, and so on. What if you want to be other than what you presently think you are? You may argue that others have been born with the special talent you lack but desire to have. This is true. But they had to cultivate the habit of that ability some time—if not in this life, then in a previous one. So whatever you want to be, start to develop that pattern now. You can instill any trend in your consciousness right now, provided you inject a strong thought in your mind; then your actions and whole being will obey that thought. Do not settle for a one-track mentality. You should be able to succeed in any profession or do anything you put your mind to. Whenever others told me I would not be able to do a thing, I made up my mind that I could do it, and I did!

Few demonstrations of mind power are more dramatic than the power of thought for good or ill on the health of the body. My Guru told me the following story: He had lost much weight as a result of a serious illness. During convalescence, he visited his guru, Lahiri Mahasaya. The Yogavatar* inquired about his health. Sri Yukteswarji explained the cause of his delicate condition.

"So," Lahiri Mahasaya said, "you made yourself sick and now you think you are thin. But I am sure you will feel better tomorrow."

The next day, Gurudeva went exultantly to Lahiri Mahasaya and proclaimed, "Sir, with your blessings, I feel much better today."

Lahiri Mahasaya responded, "Your condition was indeed quite serious, and you are still frail. Who knows how you might feel tomorrow?"

The next day Sri Yukteswarji was again completely debilitated. He lamented to his Guru, "Sir, I am again ailing. I could hardly drag myself here to you."

---

* A title given to Lahiri Mahasaya, who is revered as an avatar (divine incarnation) whose life ideally expressed the goals of yoga (science of union with God).

Lahiri Mahasaya replied, "So, once more you indispose yourself."

After some days of this alternating health and ill health, which followed exactly the expectation of Sri Yukteswarji's thoughts influenced by Lahiri Mahasaya's suggestions, my Guru realized the powerful lesson Lahiri Mahasaya had been trying to teach him.

The Yogavatar said, "What is this? One day you say to me, 'I am well,' and the next day you say, 'I am sick.' It isn't that I have been healing or indisposing you. It is your own thoughts that have made you alternately weak and strong."

Then Master said, "If I think I am well and that I have regained my former weight, will it be so?"

Lahiri Mahasaya answered, "It is so."

Guruji said, "At that very moment I felt both my strength and weight return. When I reached my mother's home that night, she was startled to see my changed condition and thought that I was swelling from dropsy. Many of my friends were so amazed at my sudden recovery that they became disciples of Lahiri Mahasaya."*

Such phenomenal demonstrations are possible to those who possess the power of realization that everything is thought. When you have yet to attain that realization, you have to keep applying will and positive affirmation until you make thought work for you. *Thought is the matrix of all creation; thought created everything.* If you hold on to that truth with indomitable will, you can materialize any thought. There is nothing that can gainsay it. It was by that kind of powerful thought that Christ rebuilt his crucified body; and it is what he referred to when he said, "Therefore I say unto you, What things soever ye desire, when ye pray, believe that ye receive them, and ye shall have them."†

* See also the account of this story in *Autobiography of a Yogi,* Chapter 12.
† Mark 11:24.

Let Nothing Weaken the Will
Behind Positive Thoughts

Once you have said, "I will," never give in. If you say, "I will never catch cold," and the next morning you have a terrible cold and are discouraged, you are allowing your will to remain weak. You must not get discouraged when you see something happening that is contrary to what you have affirmed. Keep on believing, knowing it will be so. If outwardly you say, "I will," but inwardly think, "I can't," then you neutralize the power of thought and emasculate your will. If your will has become weakened by fighting disease or other reverses, you have to take the help of someone else's will to strengthen you through their prayers and positive affirmations on your behalf. But you must also do your part to change your consciousness. That is my advice to you. Develop your will power and positive thinking, and you will find your body, mind, and soul working to mold everything in your life according to your will.

As thought is the most powerful agent in your life, provided you know how to develop and use it, never let the power of your thought be diluted by mixing with weak-minded or negative people—unless you are very strong-minded and can instead strengthen those persons. Failures should align themselves with successful people. The weak should seek the company of those who are stronger. People who have no self-control should associate with those who are self-disciplined—the greedy man, for example, should eat with the man of self-control; with such an example before him, he will begin to reason, "I also can control my appetite."

Change Your Consciousness
From Mortality to Divinity

Just as by the power of thought you can change yourself to be whatever you want to be, so most importantly, you will be able to change your consciousness from that of a

mortal to a divine being. The mortal man
is he who thinks, "This is the way I live and
this is the way I'll be until I die." But the
divine man says, "I dreamed I was a mortal,
but now I am awake and know that I am a
child of God, made in the image of the Father." Though it takes time to realize this
fully, it can be done.

If when time comes for meditation at
night you yield to the thought, "It is so late
now to meditate; let me sleep and I will
meditate tomorrow," you will be sleeping on
into the grave. When the world has surren-
dered to the drug of slumber, you be awake
in God. And throughout the day's activities,
think that it is God who is working through
you. Give the responsibility to Him. He who
thinks of God all the time, can he do wrong?
Even if he happens to err, God knows it was
his wish to do right. Give everything to God,
and you will change because then the human ego can no longer dictate to you.

No matter what comes to you, just say,

"God knows best. It is He who is giving me this suffering; it is He who is making me happy." With this attitude, all your nightmares of life will change into a beautiful dream of God.

Darkness is the absence of light. Delusion is darkness; Reality is light. Your eyes of wisdom are closed, so you see only the darkness; and you are suffering in that delusion. Change your consciousness; open your eyes and you will see in the stars the sparkle of that Divine Light. In every atom of space you will see the twinkle of God's light of laughter. Behind every thought you shall feel the ocean of His wisdom.

The dance of life and death, prosperity and failure, have no reality except as dreams of God. Realize this, and you shall see that it is materialized thoughts that are dancing around you, and that you are the ocean of thought. Nothing can stay nor hurt you.

Now I ask you to close your eyes and think of one bad habit you want to get rid of.

If you concentrate with me as I say the words in Spirit, and you believe, you shall be free of that habit. Throw away the thought that you cannot give up whatever it is. I am sending a strong thought into your consciousness that right now you are rid of that habit. Affirm with me: "I am free of that habit *now*! I am free!" Hold on to that thought of freedom; forget the bad habit. Many of you will find that the habit you have willed away will never come back again.

Repeat after me: "I shall remold my consciousness. In this new year I am a new person. And I shall change my consciousness again and again until I have driven away all the darkness of ignorance and manifested the shining light of Spirit in whose image I am made."

PARAMAHANSA YOGANANDA
(1893–1952)

"The ideal of love for God and service to humanity found full expression in the life of Paramahansa Yogananda....Though the major part of his life was spent outside India, still he takes his place among our great saints. His work continues to grow and shine ever more brightly, drawing people everywhere on the path of the pilgrimage of the Spirit."

—from a tribute by the Government of India upon issuing a commemorative stamp in Paramahansa Yogananda's honor

Born in India on January 5, 1893, Paramahansa Yogananda devoted his life to helping people of all races and creeds to realize and express more fully in their lives the true beauty, nobility, and divinity of the human spirit.

After graduating from Calcutta University in 1915, Sri Yogananda took formal vows as a monk of India's venerable monastic Swami Order. Two years later, he began his life's work with the founding of a "how-to-live" school—since grown to twenty-one educational institutions throughout India—where traditional academic subjects were offered together with yoga training and instruction in spiritual ideals. In 1920, he was invited to serve as India's delegate to an International Congress of Religious Liberals in Boston. His address to the Congress and subsequent lectures on the East Coast were enthusiastically received, and in 1924 he embarked on a cross-continental speaking tour.

Over the next three decades, Paramahansa Yogananda contributed in far-reaching ways to a greater awareness and appreciation in the West of the spiritual wisdom of the East. In Los Angeles, he established an international headquarters for Self-Realization Fellowship — the nonsectarian religious society he had founded in 1920. Through his writings, extensive lecture tours, and the creation of Self-Realization Fellowship temples and meditation centers, he introduced hundreds of thousands of truth-seekers to the ancient science and philosophy of Yoga and its universally applicable methods of meditation.

Today, the spiritual and humanitarian work begun by Paramahansa Yogananda continues under the direction of Sri Mrinalini Mata, one of his closest disciples and president of Self-Realization Fellowship/Yogoda Satsanga Society of India. In addition to publishing his writings, lectures, and informal talks (including a comprehensive series of *Self-Realization Fellowship Lessons* for home study), the society also oversees temples, retreats, and centers around the world; the monastic communities of the Self-Realization Order; and a Worldwide Prayer Circle.

In an article on Sri Yogananda's life and work,

Dr. Quincy Howe, Jr., Professor of Ancient Languages at Scripps College, wrote: "Paramahansa Yogananda brought to the West not only India's perennial promise of God-realization, but also a practical method by which spiritual aspirants from all walks of life may progress rapidly toward that goal. Originally appreciated in the West only on the most lofty and abstract level, the spiritual legacy of India is now accessible as practice and experience to all who aspire to know God, not in the beyond, but in the here and now.... Yogananda has placed within the reach of all the most exalted methods of contemplation."

How-to-Live Series
Glossary

ashram. A spiritual hermitage; often a monastery.

astral world. The subtle world of light and energy that lies behind the physical universe. Every being, every object, every vibration on the physical plane has an astral counterpart, for in the astral universe (heaven) is the "blueprint" of the material universe. A discussion of the astral world and the still subtler causal or ideational world of thought may be found in Chapter 43 of Paramahansa Yogananda's *Autobiography of a Yogi*.

Aum (Om). The Sanskrit root word or seed-sound symbolizing that aspect of Godhead which creates and sustains all things; Cosmic Vibration. *Aum* of the Vedas became the sacred word *Hum* of the Tibetans; *Amin* of the Muslims; and *Amen* of the Egyptians, Greeks, Romans, Jews, and Christians. The world's great religions state that all created things originate in the cosmic vibratory energy of *Aum* or Amen, the Word or Holy Ghost. "In the beginning was the Word, and the Word was with God, and the Word was God....All things were made by him [the Word or *Aum*]; and without him was not any thing made that was made" (John 1:1,3).

avatar. From the Sanskrit word *avatara* ("descent"), signifying the descent of Divinity into flesh. One who attains union with Spirit and then returns to earth to help humanity is called an avatar.

Bhagavad Gita. "Song of the Lord." Part of the ancient Indian *Mahabharata* epic, presented in the form of a dialogue between the avatar *(q.v.)* Lord Krishna and his disciple Arjuna. A profound treatise on the science of Yoga and a timeless prescription for happiness and success in everyday living.

Bhagavan Krishna (Lord Krishna). An avatar *(q.v.)* who lived in India many centuries before the Christian era. His teachings on Yoga *(q.v.)* are presented in the Bhagavad Gita. One of the meanings given for the word *Krishna* in the Hindu scriptures is "Omniscient Spirit." Thus, *Krishna,* like *Christ,* is a title signifying the spiritual magnitude of the avatar—his oneness with God. (See *Christ Consciousness.*)

Christ center. The center of concentration and will at the point between the eyebrows; seat of Christ Consciousness and of the spiritual eye *(q.v.)*.

Christ Consciousness. The projected consciousness of God immanent in all creation. In Christian scripture it is called the "only begotten son," the only pure reflection in creation of God the Father; in Hindu scripture it is called *Kutastha Chaitanya,* the cosmic intelligence of Spirit everywhere present in creation. It is the universal consciousness, oneness with God, manifested by Jesus, Krishna, and other avatars. Great saints and yogis know it as the state of *samadhi (q.v.)* meditation wherein their consciousness has become identified with the intelligence in every particle of creation; they feel the entire universe as their own body.

Cosmic Consciousness. The Absolute; Spirit beyond creation. Also the *samadhi*-meditation state of oneness with God both beyond and within vibratory creation.

guru. Spiritual teacher. The *Guru Gita* (verse 17) aptly describes the guru as "dispeller of darkness" (from *gu,* "darkness" and *ru,* "that which dispels"). Though the word *guru* is often misused to refer simply to any teacher or instructor, a true God-illumined guru is one who, in his attainment of self-mastery, has realized his identity with the omnipresent Spirit. Such a one is uniquely qualified to lead others on their inward spiritual journey.

The nearest English equivalent to *guru* is the word *Master.* As a mark of respect, Paramahansa Yogananda's disciples often use this term in addressing or referring to him.

karma. The effects of past actions, from this or previous lifetimes. The law of karma is that of action and reaction, cause and effect, sowing and reaping. By their thoughts and actions, human beings become the molders of their own destinies. Whatever energies a person has set into motion, wisely or unwisely, must return to that person as their starting point, like a circle inexorably completing itself. An individual's karma follows him or her from incarnation to incarnation until fulfilled or spiritually transcended. (See *reincarnation.*)

Krishna. See *Bhagavan Krishna.*

Kriya Yoga. A sacred spiritual science, originating millenniums ago in India. A form of *Raja* ("royal" or "complete") *Yoga,* it includes certain advanced techniques of meditation that lead to direct, personal experience of God. *Kriya Yoga* is explained in Chapter 26 of *Autobiography of a Yogi,* and is taught to students of the *Self-Realization Fellowship Lessons* who fulfill certain spiritual requirements.

maya. The delusory power inherent in the structure of creation, by which the One appears as many. *Maya* is the principle of relativity, inversion, contrast, duality, oppositional states; the "Satan" (lit., in Hebrew, "the adversary") of the Old Testament prophets. Paramahansa Yogananda wrote: "The Sanskrit word *maya* means 'the measurer'; it is the magical power in creation by which limitations and divisions are apparently present in the Immeasurable and Inseparable....In God's plan and play (*lila*), the sole function of Satan or *maya* is to attempt to divert man from Spirit to matter, from Reality to unreality....*Maya* is the veil of transitoriness in Nature...the veil that each man must lift in order to see behind it the Creator, the changeless Immutable, eternal Reality."

paramahansa. A spiritual title signifying one who has attained the highest state of unbroken communion with God. It may be conferred only by a true guru on a qualified disciple. Swami Sri Yukteswar bestowed the title on Paramahansa Yogananda in 1935.

reincarnation. A discussion of reincarnation may be found in Chapter 43 of Paramahansa Yogananda's *Autobiography of a Yogi.* As explained there, by the law of karma *(q.v.),* the past actions of human beings set into motion the effects that draw them back to this material plane. Through a succession of births and deaths they return to earth repeatedly to undergo here the experiences that are the fruits of those past actions, and to continue a process of spiritual evolution that leads ultimately to realization of the soul's inherent perfection and union with God.

samadhi. Spiritual ecstasy; superconscious experience; ultimately, union with God as the all-pervading supreme Reality.

Satan. See *maya.*

Self. Capitalized to denote the *atman,* or soul, the divine essence of man, as distinguished from the ordinary self, which is the human personality or ego. The Self is individualized Spirit, whose essential nature is ever-existing, ever-conscious, ever-new Bliss.

Self-realization. Realization of one's true identity as the Self, one with the universal consciousness of God. Paramahansa Yogananda wrote: "Self-realization is the knowing—in body, mind, and soul—that we are one with the omnipresence of God; that we do not have to pray that it come to us, that we are not merely near it at all times, but that God's omnipresence is our omnipresence; that we are just as much a part of Him now as we ever will be. All we have to do is improve our knowing."

spiritual eye. The single eye of intuition and spiritual perception at the Christ (*Kutastha*) center *(q.v.)* between the eyebrows; the entryway into higher states of consciousness. During deep meditation, the single or spiritual eye becomes visible as a bright star surrounded by a sphere of blue light that, in turn, is encircled by a brilliant halo of golden light. This omniscient eye is variously referred to in scriptures as the third eye, the star of the East, the inner eye, the dove descending from heaven, the eye of Shiva, and the eye of intuition. "If therefore thine eye be single, thy whole body shall be full of light" (Matthew 6:22).

Yoga. The word *Yoga* (from the Sanskrit *yuj,* "union") means union of the individual soul with Spirit; also, the methods by which this goal is attained. There are various systems of Yoga. That taught by Paramahansa Yogananda is *Raja Yoga,* the "royal" or "complete" yoga, which centers around practice of scientific methods of meditation. The sage Patanjali, foremost ancient exponent of Yoga, has outlined eight definite steps by which the *Raja Yogi* attains *samadhi,* or union with God. These are (1) *yama,* moral conduct; (2) *niyama,* religious observances; (3) *asana,* right posture to still bodily restlessness; (4) *pranayama,* control of *prana,* subtle life currents; (5) *pratyahara,* interiorization; (6) *dharana,* concentration; (7) *dhyana,* meditation; and (8) *samadhi,* superconscious experience.

BOOKS BY PARAMAHANSA YOGANANDA

Available at bookstores or online at
www.srfbooks.org

Autobiography of a Yogi

Autobiography of a Yogi
(Audiobook, read by Sir Ben Kingsley)

God Talks With Arjuna: The Bhagavad Gita—A New
Translation and Commentary

The Second Coming of Christ: The Resurrection of the
Christ Within You—A Revelatory Commentary on the
Original Teachings of Jesus

The Collected Talks and Essays

Volume I: Man's Eternal Quest

Volume II: The Divine Romance

Volume III: Journey to Self-realization

Wine of the Mystic: The Rubaiyat of Omar Khayyam—
A Spiritual Interpretation

Whispers from Eternity

DVD VIDEO

Awake: The Life of Yogananda
A film by CounterPoint Films

*A complete catalog of books and audio/video recordings
—including rare archival recordings of Paramahansa
Yogananda—is available on request or online at*
www.yogananda-srf.org.

SELF-REALIZATION FELLOWSHIP LESSONS

The scientific techniques of meditation taught by Parama-hansa Yogananda, including *Kriya Yoga* — as well as his guidance on all aspects of balanced spiritual living — are presented in the *Self-Realization Fellowship Lessons.* A free introductory booklet, *Undreamed-of Possibilities*, is available on our website www.yogananda-srf.org.

SELF-REALIZATION FELLOWSHIP
3880 San Rafael Avenue • Los Angeles, CA 90065-3219
TEL (323) 225-2471 • FAX (323) 225-5088

Also published by Self-Realization Fellowship...

AUTOBIOGRAPHY OF A YOGI
by Paramahansa Yogananda

This acclaimed autobiography presents a fascinating portrait of one of the great spiritual figures of our time. With engaging candor, eloquence, and wit, Paramahansa Yogananda narrates the inspiring chronicle of his life — the experiences of his remarkable childhood, encounters with many saints and sages during his youthful search throughout India for an illumined teacher, ten years of training in the hermitage of a revered yoga master, and the thirty years that he lived and taught in America. Also recorded here are his meetings with Mahatma Gandhi, Rabindranath Tagore, Luther Burbank, the Catholic stigmatist Therese Neumann, and other celebrated spiritual personalities of East and West.

Autobiography of a Yogi is at once a beautifully written account of an exceptional life and a profound introduction to the ancient science of Yoga and its time-honored tradition of meditation. The author clearly explains the subtle but definite laws behind both the ordinary events of everyday life and the extraordinary events commonly termed miracles. His absorbing life story thus becomes the background for a penetrating and unforgettable look at the ultimate mysteries of human existence.

Considered a modern spiritual classic, the book has been translated into more than forty languages and is widely used as a text and reference work in colleges and universities. A perennial bestseller since it was first published more than sixty years ago, *Autobiography of a Yogi* has found its way into the hearts of millions of readers around the world.

An award-winning documentary film about Paramahansa Yogananda's life and work, *Awake: The Life of Yogananda*, was released in October 2014.

———————————————

"A rare account." — THE NEW YORK TIMES

"A fascinating and clearly annotated study."
— NEWSWEEK

"There has been nothing before, written in English or in any other European language, like this presentation of Yoga."
— COLUMBIA UNIVERSITY PRES

By the Editors of Consumer Guide®

(Medical Book of Remedies)

50 WAYS TO EASE BACK PAIN

In Association with the
TEXAS BACK INSTITUTE

BILLY GLISAN, M.S.
Consultant: Stephen Hochschuler, M.D.

Publications International, Ltd.